Christian Kimmich

Electricity supply for irrigation

Agricultural policies and farm level economics

Emerging megacities
Dicussion Papers
Edited by Konrad Hagedorn, Christine Werthmann, Dimitrios Zikos, Ramesh Chennamaneni

Humboldt-Universität zu Berlin
Department of Agricultural Economics
Division of Resource Economics
Philippstr. 13, House 12
10115 Berlin

Tel.: +49 (0)30 2093 6305
Fax: +49 (0)30 2093 6497
www.agrar.hu-berlin.de/struktur/institute/wisola/fg/ress
www.sustainable-hyderabad.de

Contact: emerging.megacities@hu-berlin.de

The emerging megacities discussion papers are available at:
www.eh-verlag.de

ISSN print edition 2193-6927

Emerging megacities Discussion Papers are prepared by researchers working on topics in the realm of sustainable development in Megacities of Tomorrow, a research priority by the German Ministry of Education and Research (BMBF). The papers have been peer-reviewed by a board of external reviewers.
Views and opinions expressed do not necessarily represent those of the Division of Resource Economics.
Comments are highly welcome and should be sent directly to the authors.
We welcome contributions on any topics related to Megacities of Tomorrow. Further information on the submission procedure is given at:
www.sustainable-hyderabad.de/emerging-megacities

Kimmich, Christian

Electricity supply for irrigation
Agricultural policies and farm level economics

Emerging megacities Discussion Papers, Volume 2/2010

ISBN/EAN: 978-3-86741-819-5

First published in 2012 by Europaeischer Hochschulverlag GmbH & Co KG, Bremen, Germany.

© Europaeischer Hochschulverlag GmbH & Co KG, Fahrenheitstr. 1, D-28359 Bremen (www.eh-verlag.de). All rights reserved.

Cover: Photo "Metropolis", ferendus (flickr). Creative Commons License

No part of this publication may be reproduced or transmitted, in any form or by any means, electronic, mechanical, photocopying, recording or otherwise, or stored in any retrieval system of nay nature, without the written permission of the copyright holder and the publisher, application for which shall be made to the publisher.

EHV

Electricity supply for irrigation
Agricultural policies and farm level economics

*Christian Kimmich**

July 2010

Abstract

This report focuses on the policies of electricity provision for irrigation and the cost of groundwater-based irrigation. The empirical findings indicate that electricity regulation is unlikely to fulfil the expectations of an allocation-efficient tariff structure in the given political situation, leading to regulatory capture. The report's chronological approach reveals development paths that are also present in the current action situations. The findings suggest that the involved properties of transactions inherent in the choices available to each actor are constitutive for understanding the unfolding of each potential and the realised development path. The economic conditions of dry-land agriculture and the costs of food provision render a shift towards a cost-based tariff setting unlikely.

The analysis at the level of electricity distribution and agricultural production systems indicates that although marginal costs of electricity supply are inexistent, the costs for the consequences of poor infrastructure incur heavy burdens on agricultural enterprises. The costs of electricity would exceed those for each of the other input factors of production. The absence of marginal costs has led to highly inefficient groundwater irrigation. Fortunately, incentives in agriculture for higher power quality are given, resulting from the high costs of pump set burnouts through voltage fluctuations. This incentive can be combined with energy efficiency measures. Effective measures are most feasible at the level of the electricity sub-station, isolating an agricultural electricity feeder and the connected distribution transformers.

Key words: *electricity-irrigation nexus, agricultural policy, production economics, Andhra Pradesh, India*

---

* Tel.: +49 30 2093 6430. Email: christian.kimmich@staff.hu-berlin.de, Division of Resource Economics, Humboldt Universität zu Berlin, Philippstraße 13, 10099 Berlin

1 Outline

Agriculture is a crucial sector either enabling or impeding a transition path towards a sustainable development of urban areas. This is also the case for the emerging megacity of Hyderabad. Several rural-urban linkages support this perspective: (a) The migration patterns, being heavily interlinked with both sector-wise and rural development paths, (b) the food security and provisioning dimension, being especially relevant in the case of perishable agricultural commodities which cannot be traded over long distances, (c) water allocation for agricultural production versus drinking water supply in the city, and (d) power allocation for agricultural production versus urban consumption. This research focuses especially on the latter linkage, as electricity provision is one of the most crucial factors of sustainable development for the emerging megacity, becoming either a driver or inhibitor.

Electricity for agricultural irrigation is subsidised in Andhra Pradesh, where precipitation is highly uncertain and where water builds the bottleneck for agricultural production. The subsidisation policy has led to a heavy increase in electric energy demand, an alarming level of groundwater depletion and financial burdens (World Bank 2001). As a consequence, high electric energy demand for agricultural irrigation has reduced the supply for industrial, commercial and household purposes and impedes economic development in these sectors.

This report addresses two fundamental research questions. One aims at the agricultural policy level (Section 2), the other at the economics at the farm level (Section 3):

- What are the reasons for electricity subsidisation and are there regulatory governance or policy approaches towards addressing the related energy inefficiencies?
- What are the implications on the level of agricultural enterprises and which approaches are feasible at this level?

2 Infrastructure regulation and the political economy of the electricity-irrigation nexus in agriculture

Subsidisation[1] of energy for agricultural irrigation is a widespread phenomenon in many countries worldwide. The semi-arid and arid regions of India play an eminent role in

---

[1] The term 'subsidisation' is here defined as any monetary cost created which is not born by the beneficiary of the transacted good. The analysed agricultural subsidisation does not include other input costs and impacts on the prices of agricultural commodities, which has in fact led to a net

this regard, where precipitation is highly unbalanced and water an extremely scarce, yet elementary factor in agricultural production. The subsidisation has led to twofold resource use inefficiencies: A heavy increase in electric energy demand (Das 2007) and an alarming level of groundwater depletion (Scott and Shah 2004). In India, the policy of subsidising agricultural electricity provision started in the early 1980s in the state of Andhra Pradesh (AP). It not only contributed to environmental degradation, but also to financial burdens of the electric utilities and the states' budget (World Bank 2001).

India faced a severe foreign exchange crisis in 1991 that could only be encountered with credits by the International Monetary Fund (IMF). The pace of restructuring the Indian economy had to be enhanced (Rothermund 1993). In order to balance its budget, the government increased divestment of public enterprises. This was supposed to include even utilities that, until recently, had been argued to be necessarily public because of their 'natural monopoly' properties, such as electricity. After a failed policy to introduce competition through private Independent Power Producers (IPP), India re-oriented its policy towards independent regulation and the organisational segregation of electricity generation, transmission and distribution in order to prepare for privatisation (Dubash and Rajan 2000). State Electricity Regulatory Commissions (SERC) were set-up from 1998 onwards, partly to reduce political interference and phase out subsidisation.

The electricity subsidies were supposed to increase production, to support agricultural groups and to secure their income. Yet, the outcomes of this policy became increasingly problematic. Due to the financial constraints of the electric utilities, power generation could not keep pace with the increase in electric energy consumption. Power quality could no longer be maintained as the distribution grid was not prepared to carry the high and variable demand. The extreme voltage fluctuations led to regular motor burnouts, scheduled power-cuts and unscheduled blackouts and made time-constrained irrigation difficult (Tongia 2007). As it seems, the policy had navigated the electric utilities and agriculture into a dilemma situation of lock-in. A World Bank (2001) research, conducted from 1998 to 2001, found that both parties, the utilities and the farmers, would be better off with cost-based electricity tariffs in exchange for adequate quality of electricity. However, the prevailing policy seems to support mainly medium and large farms, where the fixed cost of investment in pumps is relatively smaller (Modi 2005). Yet, two elections later, no change is in sight.

---

taxation for several time periods (quote). What is more, this term only covers market-transacted costs and does not include any other transactions (i.e. 'externalities').

How can this development be explained from an economic and political perspective? Can economic and political theory contribute to understanding the history of this process and the current situation? If this is the case, can there be a contribution that possibly gives guidance to where a chance of unlocking the current dilemma might be found? How did agricultural electricity subsidisation emerge? Why is agricultural electricity subsidisation so persistent, even though it heavily contributes to fiscal deficits and resource degradation? What has been the impact of the introduction of independent regulation on the electricity utilities and the agricultural electricity provision?

2.1 Literature review: utilities regulation and regulatory agencies

Profound applied research has been conducted on the Indian case, covering the impacts on irrigation and groundwater depletion (Scott and Shah 2004), the impacts on energy consumption and power quality (World Bank 2001), electricity regulation and policies (Dubash and Rao 2008) and the political economy and history of subsidisation (Birner et al. 2007, Fan, Gulati and Thorat 2007, Kale 2004).

How infrastructure is governed seems to be most crucial with regards to economic outcomes for related stakeholders. The involved actors include the end-users of infrastructure, the utilities, the regulator and the government. Basically, three relationships can be characterised in regulation: The relation between (1) the regulator and regulated utilities, between (2) government and regulator, and between (3) the public and the government, mediated through political parties and interest groups. These relationships also seem to be the most crucial in understanding the regulatory choices and policies that have been made in the past. The related theories on utilities regulation and regulatory agencies will be reviewed in this sub-section.

The transaction cost approach towards understanding economic organisation is based on selected physical attributes of the involved transactions and some general assumptions on human behaviour, i.e. opportunistic behaviour and bounded rationality. It created a whole research agenda, that, to an important extent, also covers the network industries (Shelanski and Klein 1995). Using the transaction cost approach, the transaction costs of vertical separation versus integration and related regulation can be assessed. However, making a general assumption about human behaviour leads to serious doubts about the value of the theory (Ghoshal and Moran 1996). Even a derivative of this theory, the alleged dichotomy of hierarchy and market, with hybrid governance in between, seems problematic: "By sticking to the twin pillars of markets and hierarchies, our attention is deflected from a diversity of organisational designs that are [...] a distinctly different form" (Powell 1991: 290). The three essential transaction relations proposed by Commons (1936) would also suggest a rather triadic perspective that I will further elaborate on in the subsequent section.

Game theory has only lately influenced research in regulatory economics. Depending on the assumptions of rationality, it can predict how agents behave according to the choices that are available to them. Although precision of rigorous modelling is limited, "the approach offers insights that can be checked against history and evidence" (Newbery 1999: 30). It includes the set of available actions, strategies and information and the resulting payoffs to determine outcomes and equilibria. In its simplest form, the regulation game includes the regulator and the utility. However, unions, judiciary, politicians, consumer, environmental and other interest groups can also affect payoffs and are crucial for understanding the regulatory outcomes. Hence, they should be reflected in empirically based games. Newbery (1999) also describes the laws and acts that have an influence on the set of actions available to the regulator. He further elaborates on the role of credible commitment, a theme that is further dealt with below.

Regulatory agencies[2] are created by legislation, with elected officials as their principals. They are organisationally separated and headed by usually unelected commissioners. They receive the power and responsibility under public law to regulate their field, but are subject to the scrutiny and control of elected politicians, ministries and judges. Hence, the delegation decisively exceeds consultative tasks. From a transaction cost perspective, delegation to regulators can be seen as a delegation of complex, often technical decisions to specialists with scientific expertise, reducing costs, information asymmetries, but also agency losses. Credible commitment is usually seen as the most crucial function of delegated regulation. Predictable commitment enables capital-intensive investments of economic actors, as it increases the security of investments and related returns in the regulated sector (Newbery 1999). Credible commitment towards voters and organised interest groups enables distributional, partial and impartial public interests, and creates economic or political benefits for the elected officials. The notion of independence is often not further differentiated. Usually, a distinction between two relations is made: (a) the independence from political influences, and (b) the independence from partial economic interests of the regulated. A third independence, (c) the independence to regulate, i.e. the ability to regulate, is usually dealt with under the notion of regulatory

---

[2] Thatcher (2002) analyses a broad variety of regulatory agencies, including utility regulators, competition authorities, financial bodies, bodies for media independence, privacy, food safety, environmental protection, gender equity, or against racial discrimination.

discretion. Political sciences describes regulators as non-majoritarian institutions (NMI) where democratic legitimacy is an important issue (Thatcher 2002).

2.2 A theoretical framework for analysis

Today, some elaborated analytical frameworks to approach the political economy are available. The advocacy coalition framework (Sabatier 2007), actor-centred institutionalism (Scharpf 1997), the Institutional Analysis and Development (IAD) framework (Ostrom 2005), and the Institutions of Sustainability (IoS) (Hagedorn 2008) all provide a composition of interrelated perspectives that can drive analysis. I will draw from these perspectives with a special focus on transactions and choices.

Transactions have been at the core of economic analysis for a while. While classical institutionalism mainly focused on the institutional dimensions of transactions, later perspectives increasingly emphasised the physical dimensions and their interrelation with institutions. The institutional typology of Commons (1931) and the physical typology of Hagedorn (2008) seem to be most promising in this regard.

Commons identified three fundamental negotiable transactions in economics: (i) The coercive and persuasive bargaining transactions (ii) the argumentative and pleading rationing transactions and (iii) the managerial transactions of command and obedience. He derived these from the three social relations of conflict, dependence and order that are implicit in every transaction (Commons 1931).

Hagedorn argues for an analytic distinction between (i) attributes of physical entities and how they shape (ii) the properties of transactions and (iii) the institutional dimension of transactions. The attributes can be structured along the two dimensions of (a) modularity and decomposability of structures and (b) the functional interdependence of processes. As emphasised by Hagedorn, even man-made, designed systems can reveal complex-interconnected transactions (Hagedorn 2008). This is especially relevant for infrastructure, as the case of electricity infrastructure and the related governance structures reveal. The interrelation of physical attributes and related economic organisation of electricity has hardly been explicitly dealt with. An exception is Wilson (2002).

2.3 Empirics and discussion

As electricity governance, according to the Indian Constitution, is a 'concurrent' subject of the Nation and its States, it is crucial to focus on state policies. As mentioned, the changing regulation in the electricity sector, including unbundling and the introduction of an electricity regulatory commission, was hoped to increase regulatory independence and to allow setting the tariffs more 'rationally' (Bhattacharyya 2005). Related to gestation costs, agricultural electricity tariffs would hence increase. The change in governance had been proposed on the basis of similar developments in other countries. Regulatory independence was then proposed by the World Bank, and after a first experiment in Orissa it was also incorporated in the Andhra Pradesh Electricity Reform Act, 1998 and later on at the national level within the Electricity Act, 2003.

The Indian history did not always know a political environment of subsidising agriculture. It is helpful to go back to the time when electricity governance was shaped and electric pump sets for irrigation became broadly used. This offers an understanding of the circumstances, under which the subsidisation of electricity could emerge and helps to understand the current situation and the path-dependencies and lock-in situations that have emerged.

2.3.1 Early electricity infrastructure regulation and provision to agriculture

Immediately after independence, India redrafted its law for electricity, the Electricity (Supply) Act, 1948 that prepared the creation of a Central Electricity Authority and the State Electricity Boards. Like the preceding Indian Electricity Act, 1910, this was supported by experts from the United Kingdom where similar acts had been legislated before (Bhattacharyya 2005). Conventional wisdom at that time saw electricity as a crucial factor of economic development that was supposed to be publicly owned, a position that became formalised in the Industrial Policy Resolution 1956 (Bhattacharyya 2005). This policy was supported by industrialists in the country, as electricity required large capital investment. Also rural interest advocated nationalisation, as the expansion of infrastructure into rural areas would not be profitable for private utilities. Electricity became an important political instrument for subsidisation. Until the early 1970s, the industry received electricity at a significantly lower tariff than other consumers. Rural interests were much less powerful (Kale 2004). In 1960, there were merely 13,000 agricultural electricity services that had been connected to the grid in AP (APTRANSCO 2008). Ten years later, this number had already increased by ten times (see Figure 1). In 1970, Indian agriculture consumed roughly ten percent of all electricity. Industries were by far the most important electricity consumers in India with a share of 67% (CMIE 2008: 132).

In 1980, agriculture already contributed to nearly twenty percent of all electricity consumed in Andhra Pradesh (see Figure 2), roughly twice as much as domestic and

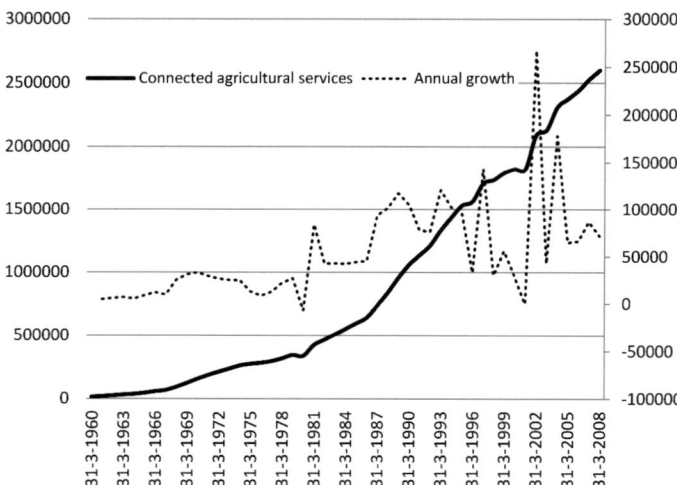

Figure 1: Connected agricultural services in Andhra Pradesh
Source: APTRANSCO (2008)

commercial consumers. These numbers have to be interpreted cautiously however. The seemingly sharp decline of agricultural electricity consumption in 1996 does not stem from a real regression but rather a correction of the accounting practices of the electricity utilities[3]. This correction originates from an institutional change towards independent regulation, which took shape after the Indian debt crisis in 1991.

In 1983, the policy of flat-rate electricity tariffs for agricultural groundwater irrigation was first introduced. This had a tremendous impact on the number of newly connected pump-sets with an annual growth rate of eleven percent till 1990. Till today, this has resulted in an annual growth rate of seven percent in connections. From 1980, the electricity consumption increased with an annually growth rate of close to thirteen percent. Electricity consumption outpaced the number of connected pump-sets, indicating an increasing consumption per pump-set. In 2007, the share of agriculture in total electricity consumption stood at 36 % in AP with an average of 6,460 kWh consumed per pump-set (APTRANSCO 2008, CMIE 2008).

---

[3] "According to the Campaign Coordinator of the Lok Satta, Dr. Jayaprakash Narayan, the State Electricity Board estimates of transmission and distribution (T&D) losses have been changed at will. For instance, the T&D losses for the year 1998-99 were initially shown to be 31.8 % but the figure had been later revised to 38.1 %." (The Hindu Business Line 2000, June 28)

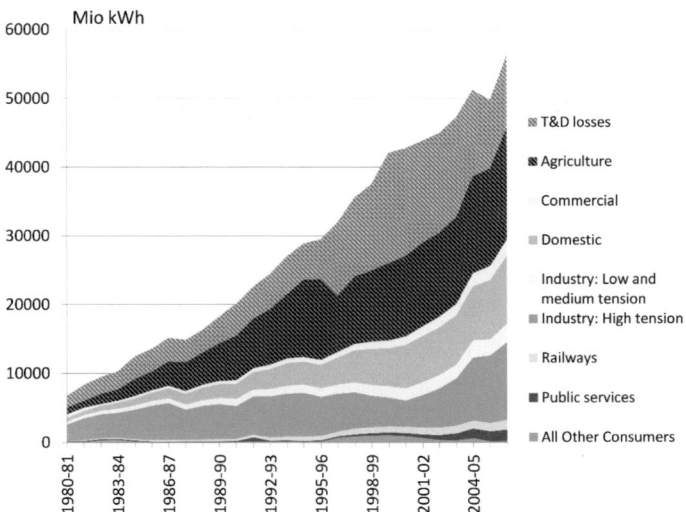

Figure 2: Electric energy consumption in Andhra Pradesh
Source: CMIE (2008: 246)

2.3.2 The emergence of agricultural electricity subsidisation

How could such an enduring regime of shifting electricity subsidisation towards agriculture unfold? As the empirical literature indicates, only an understanding of several interlinked conditions, contingencies, causes and reasons can shed light into this case.

The quest for self-sufficiency in food supply surely stipulated this dynamic. The Green Revolution brought seed varieties, which could drastically increase yields, if input factors were to be increased as well. Water and fertilisers became the 'steering wheel' towards optimal specific intensity. Another important advantage of groundwater irrigation was the reduced dependence on the vagaries and uncertainty of the monsoon, creating instead a more manageable risk. Canal irrigation could provide water only at a higher infrastructure cost in a much longer time span (Kalra, Shekhar and Shrivastava 2007), while reducing precipitation uncertainty only to a lesser extent. However, certain preconditions had to be met to provide for electricity-based groundwater irrigation: Large areas of rural India had to be electrified. The Rural Electrification Corporation was established in 1969, with the support of the World Bank. The main focus was on agricultural electricity supply (Kalra, Shekhar and Shrivastava 2007). The pace of rural electrification decreased in the 1990s and additional programs for rural households were added, with the most recent program set up in 2005 (Bhattacharyya and Srivastava 2009).

One of the main reasons for subsidisation was to enable intensification and security of agricultural production through the spread of groundwater irrigation. Only an input-linked subsidisation would support this outcome. The possibly easiest way to induce an increase in production intensity is along the electricity grid, as no additional transaction costs beyond the grid-infrastructure for the country-wide distribution would be required. In 1980, this meant reaching 340,000 agricultural electricity connections. This outcome would certainly benefit agriculture. The effected farms could achieve higher yields, hence increased food security and a higher turn-over for their commodities.

What would be the preferred outcome for the utilities? As long as subsidies are not born by them, what could be a reason to counteract? One reason could be the increased load on the electricity grid through the subsidisation, which would require further investments. But the rural electricity infrastructure has been mainly financed by the Rural Electricity Corporation (REC), which would incur hardly any costs to the transmission and distribution operator. There is, however, one reason which is discussed in the literature to have supported the subsidisation path: The costs of managing an increasing number of meters and bills of agricultural consumers and the related costs of maintaining and monitoring personnel became overwhelming in relation to the derived revenues (Scott and Shah 2004).

Yet, there is one question dominating the aforementioned calculations: Did the utilities anyhow have an incentive for cost reduction at this time? The utilities were supposed to achieve a rate of return of three percent (Rao 2004). However, this goal was never really enforced, as even the regulator as the principal of the utilities and the agent of the government did not have strong incentives to generate revenues. Budgeting constraints were actually low for the government itself, as will be shown in the subsequent section.

Finally, two general advantages of this strategy for the government will be outlined. (1) The government can increase production intensity through cross-subsidisation and hence save its own budget, and (2) this approach is also less transparent and hence conceals accountability of the government (Crew and Kleindorfer 2002).

2.3.3 The political economy dimension of subsidisation

With a look at the broader phenomenon of agricultural subsidisation, it will become obvious that not only electricity transformed into a medium of input intensification:

> *In the 1960s, irrigation accounted for more than 50 percent of the total subsidies, credit accounted for 30 percent, and power for the rest. During the*

second half of the 1970s, fertiliser subsidy became dominant, accounting for more than 50 percent of the total. Since 1982, power subsidy has taken the largest share. In 1999 it accounted for 64 percent of total input subsidies in Indian agriculture. (Fan, Gulati and Thorat 2007: 7)

Also the aggregated figure of subsidies compared to the aggregated investments in agricultural research and infrastructure offers a clear picture (see Figure 3).

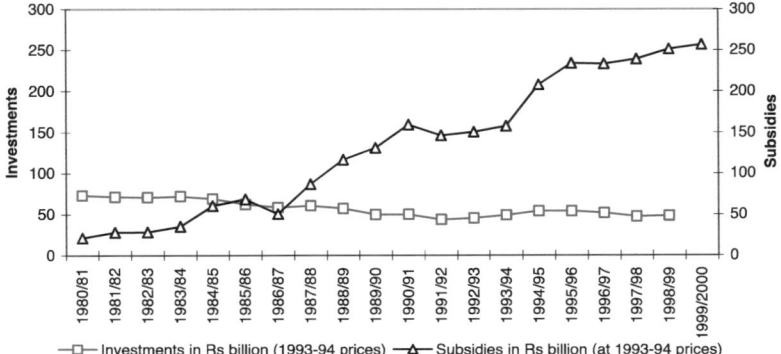

Figure 3: Input subsidies and public investments in agriculture
Source: Fan et al. (2007: 8)

Hence, there must be some reasons beyond electricity governance, which led to this pattern of subsidisation. Certainly, the governance and related transactions of irrigation, credit and fertiliser provision play a crucial role for the dominance of one subsidy over the other and also a simultaneous provision is required to prevent bottlenecks in production. Yet, the aggregated account points at a different, common denominator for this development path: Improving the immediate economic conditions of agriculture. Why would a government support agriculture with this outcome in mind?

Already in 1967, the Congress Party split and roughly at the same time new political movements emerged, some of them representing large farmers (Suri 2002). For the first time after independence the Congress Party received competition, but, although "it faced competition from local parties and some local versions of the Socialists, Communists, and the right wing, its position was assured by its ability to control resources at the national level and distribute them strategically." (Chhibber and Kollman 2004: 88). In the 1980s, a process of power shift towards the States took shape, challenging the dirigiste central government and the one-party dominant system. "In the 1980s, (..) opposition chief ministers tried to build a coalition of opposition party states—of 'Non-Congress CMs'—challenging the hegemony of the dominant party and what they termed 'the centralised state'." (Sinha 2004: 33). In order to maintain power, state governments steadily shifted their subsidisation policy towards the farmers (Kale 2004). First, a flat-rate monthly tariff was introduced delinking the price from consumption. Today, agricultural electricity supply is almost completely subsidised with a symbolic price of 20 Rs. per month.

2.4 Conclusions and practical implications

There are at least three factors that have enabled a policy change towards subsidising agricultural electricity provision: (1) The high dependence of intensive agriculture on predictable water supply, (2) the crucial factor located in the characteristics of the electricity infrastructure which requires regulation and at the same time allows for political influence and (3) the emergence of party competition which led to a 'political race' for 'vote banks'.

It has been shown that the involved transactions inherent in the choices available to each actor are constitutive for understanding the unfolding of each development path. The case of governing infrastructure with its idiosyncratic properties of transaction renders this obvious. In a polity of party competition, the political steering can become a search process that is constrained and deliberated by transactions that lead to the benefits of a majority. This is demonstrated in the studied case.

The results indicate that electricity regulation is unlikely to fulfil the expectations of an allocation-efficient tariff structure in the given political situation, leading to regulatory capture. The chronological approach reveals development paths that are also present in the current action situations. The economic conditions of dry-land agriculture and the costs of food provision render a shift towards a cost-based tariff setting unlikely. With regards to improving the infrastructure governance and energy efficiency, an analysis of the micro-level of economic organisation reveals further insights. This is the subject of the subsequent section.

3 Farm level economics: The cumulative causation of energy inefficiency

The regime of subsidised electricity provision in Indian agriculture has had a tremendous impact on the diffusion of groundwater-driven irrigation. With an average annual growth of seven percent in connections since 1980 and a growth of 13 % in electricity consumption, agriculture in AP had a share of 36 % of all electricity consumed in 2007 (CMIE 2008: 246), hence causing more than one third of all GHG emissions in electricity generation. The Indian average share of electricity consumption in 2007 stood at 22 % (CMIE 2008: 133). The drastic increase has not been the only consequence. The policy also led to a steady deterioration of the electricity infrastructure provision. Although being compensated for agricultural electricity supply by the state, the distribution companies have steadily reduced investments, maintenance and staff budgets for rural distribution. This resulted in reduced monitoring capacities, grid maintenance, high voltage fluctuations and increasing transformer burn-out rates. A large share of the transmission and distribution (T&D) losses, standing at 19 % of all electricity generated in 2007 (CMIE 2008: 245), can be ascribed to agricultural electricity provision. Yet, as meters are not used, the exact amounts are not measurable.

The poor conditions of the electricity grid also lead to high rates of motor burnouts in agricultural pump-sets. Unbranded and locally manufactured pump-sets, in combination with unqualified repairs, increase the electric inefficiency. Furthermore, farmers have to invest in grid connections, maintenance and transformer repairs, as the distribution companies retract from servicing agriculture. This cumulative causation of energy inefficiency and increasing maintenance costs for agricultural electricity provision led to a situation, where the need for a change in governance is urgent.

This part of the report focuses on the conditions of electricity provision on the ground, covering the electric distribution from the companies' sub-stations through the distribution transformers (DTR) up to the farmers' pump sets. Especially, local interaction and emerging informal governance structures will be investigated. The guiding research questions are: How is electricity provision governed at the local level between the distribution companies and agriculture? Which incentives and respective contingencies prevail for electricity-driven irrigation? How can a transition towards a sustainable development path best be facilitated?

First, the methodology will be outlined. Second, the data will be analysed structured along operationalised research questions. Third, conclusions and implications for capacity development and pilot projects will be drawn.

3.1 Methods

According to the objective of analysing the farm economics for irrigation, a survey seems to be the most useful for gaining empirical knowledge. Many interactions and arrangements can best be identified through open questions in interviews. However, basic data on agricultural cropping, irrigation and electricity utilisation patterns are best covered through standardised survey questions. Hence, the following method structure has been set-up:

- Standardised farm-level survey with N=305 and 52 survey items
- Standardised village-level survey with N=18 and 29 survey items

3.1.1 Sampling procedure

The four districts adjacent to Hyderabad have been chosen as the universe for the analysis. Based on the demographic Census data of 2001 and the village directory of the Census 2001 (Census of India 2001), a stratified village sample selection has been conducted. Two Mandals[4] in each district and in each Mandal two villages have been chosen for analysis.

Figure 4: Map of the selected districts in Andhra Pradesh
Source: own illustration based on http://en.wikipedia.org/wiki/Andhra_Pradesh

---

[4] "As part of the decentralisation of the administrative system set up in 1986, each district is divided into a number of Mandals (intermediate territorial and administrative unit, with a population of about 50,000 to 70,000 between the village and district levels) and Gram Panchayats (village councils or the area that falls under a village council)." (Suri 2002: 5)

3.1.2 Farm-level and village-level survey design

The village-level survey included items of land holding size and caste composition. This has been the basis for a representative stratification of farm-level surveys. In each village, an average of 17 farmers have been surveyed, resulting in N=305 schedules. The village-level survey included (a) general items on household, holding and caste profile, (b) cropping and irrigation patterns, (c) specific items on groundwater, bore-wells and pump sets, (d) items on village electricity provision, and (e) on surface irrigation reservoirs.

The farmers have been selected randomly, based on the stratification criteria. The head of the farm household has been selected purposefully. According to the gender ratio in farm household heads of each village, a share of female farmers has been interviewed. The farm-level survey covered (a) land holding, cropping, livestock and machinery items, (b) groundwater, bore-well and pump set items, (c) electricity provision items, (d) surface irrigation items, (e) items on agricultural training, associations, and (f) general household and demography items, as well as (g) items on financial status and credit provision.

3.2 Results and discussion

The energy consumption patterns are heavily influenced by the economic incentives, as well as the agronomic conditions. Along with the policy of electricity subsidisation, several other contingencies exist. For the research questions to become operational, the following steps will be taken:

- What are the actually incurred costs of electricity-driven irrigation within the agricultural production systems?
- Given the rapid growth of connections and electricity consumption for irrigation, what is the average consumption and costs of electricity per pump set?
- Which energy- and cost-efficient solutions are feasible and can be translated into capacity development measures and pilot projects?

3.2.1 The actual costs of electricity-driven groundwater irrigation

For an understanding of the economic incentives of the farm an analysis of the actual costs generated by cropping patterns and the respective irrigation system is crucial. For this purpose, the survey has covered the following variables:

Table 1: Summary statistics for the costs of production

Variable	Obs.	Mean	SD	Min	Max
Farm size (acres)	305	4.13	6.43	0	60
Acres irrigated by groundwater	305	3.99	4.53	0	42
Seed costs per year (Rs.)	305	5,977	6,732	400	49,000
Fertiliser and pesticide costs (Rs.)	305	4,518	4,083	167	34,335
Drilling costs (Rs.)	300	23,169	18,682	0	150,000
Pump-set costs (Rs.)	303	22,343	8,998	2,000	72,000
Connection charge (Rs.)	298	7,180	8,742	0	100,000
Connection charge, informal (Rs.)	300	946	1,456	0	10,000
Interest rate on credits taken	276	.192	.137	.03	.8

Source: calculations based on the survey

Given the year of drilling the bore, a recovery period of 20 years is derived. For the costs of the pump set, a recovery period of 15 years is derived. The costs for connecting to the electricity grid will be set to 20 years, as the replacement of a pump set does not require a new connection. Given the average interest rate of 19.2 % (see Table 1), the annuity is calculated. This results in the following costs for groundwater irrigation:

Table 2: Summary statistics for the costs of production

Type of cost	Rs.
Annuity bore	4,531
Annuity pump-set	4,600
Annuity connection	1,608
Maintenance	414
Pump-set repair	5,412
DTR repair	547
Total	17,112
Acres irrigated by groundwater	3.99
Costs of irrigation / acre	4,284.56

Source: calculations based on the survey

With an average cost of 4,285 Rs. per acre, the costs of irrigation are only slightly below the costs for fertilisers and pesticides (4,518 Rs.) and the costs for seeds (5,977 Rs.).

The costs for pump set repairs contribute the highest share to the overall costs of groundwater irrigation. With 48 %, a very high share of farmers uses locally manufactured (assembled) and no-name motors for their pump sets.

3.2.2 Energy consumption patterns for electricity-driven irrigation at the farm level

The dynamics in annual additional connections and electric energy consumption can be translated into consumption per connection or pump set. This yields a first indicator of consumption patterns at the farm level (see Figure 5).

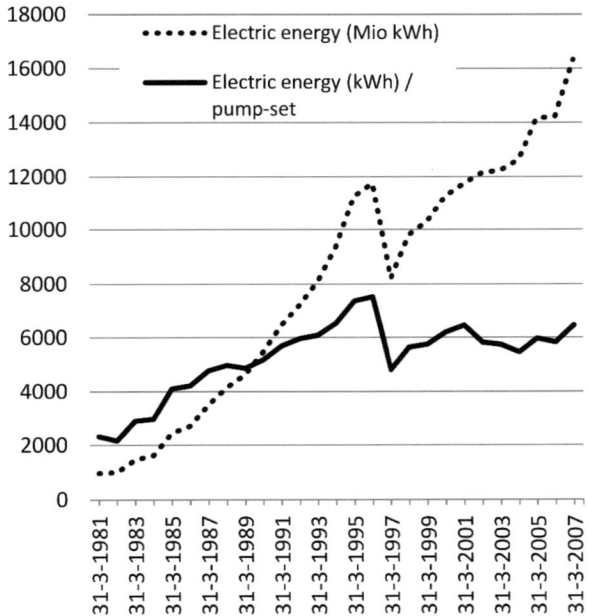

Figure 5: Electric energy consumption per pump set in Andhra Pradesh
Source: based on CMIE (2008)

The consumption per pump set has stabilised at around 6,000 kWh per year since the early 1990s. Based on the regulations of the Electricity Regulatory Commission, the tariff for agricultural connections (Low Tension Tariff No. 5) is set to 1.18 Rs. per kWh (APERC 2009: 118). This represents the amount the government pays to the Distribution Companies for electricity provision to agriculture. The average costs per pump set would then be 7,080 Rs., more than the costs for the bore well and pump set itself and the costs for fertilisers, pesticides and seeds.

3.2.3 Energy provision and saving measures

Electricity provision and energy efficiency highly depend on the type of pump set used, as well as whether the pump set is ISI-marked[5] or BEE-rated[6]. Furthermore, a capacitor can increase energy efficiency by 20-25 % (Mohan and Sreekumar 2009). With regards to power quality and quantity, a preference item has been included in the survey. The interviewee could decide between the preference for a certain time of supply (time preference), continuous supply or reduced voltage fluctuations. The following variables have been generated for this purpose:

Table 3: Energy efficiency summary statistics

Variable	Obs.	Mean	SD	Min	Max
Capacitor installed (1=yes)	305	.111	.315	0	1
Pump set manufacturer (0=no-name / locally assembled; 1 = branded)	305	.534	.500	0	1
ISI-marked (1=yes)	305	.367	.483	0	1
BEE-rated (1=yes)	305	.0557	.230	0	1
Time preference (1=yes)	305	.0918	.289	0	1
Continuous supply (1=yes)	305	.0721	.259	0	1
Voltage fluctuations (1=yes)	305	.643	.480	0	1

Source: calculations based on the survey

A capacitor is hardly used. Only 11 % of the farmers have mentioned to have a capacitor installed on their pump sets. However, even this number is doubtful. Only 53.4 % use a pump set manufactured by a known producer. Almost half of the farmers use a pump set which is locally manufactured and/or has no name. This is also reflected in the results for ISI marks. Only 36.7 % are actually marked. However, at least 5.6 % use a motor which, is BEE-rated.

Concerning the preference in electricity provision, reduced voltage fluctuation has the highest priority in the preference order of the farmers, with 64 % of the answers. Time preference (9.2 %) and continuous power supply (7.2 %) are much less important.

---

[5] The ISI standard mark is issued by the Bureau of Indian Standards (BIS) and assures that a product conforms to certain quality requirements according to the specification.
[6] The Bureau of Energy Efficiency (BEE) has developed a star-rated energy efficiency label which can be used with all electric appliances.

3.3 Conclusions and practical implications

This analysis at the level of electricity distribution and agricultural production systems indicates that although marginal costs of electricity supply being inexistent, the costs for the consequences of poor infrastructure incur heavy burdens on agricultural enterprises. The motor burnouts resulting from high voltage fluctuations lead to repair costs at an average of 5,412 Rs. per year, exceeding the costs for fertilisers and pesticides. The costs of repairing the distribution transformer incur an additional burden to the agricultural enterprises.

Derived from total electricity provision for agriculture, the total of agricultural electricity connections and the marginal costs of power supply calculated by the Regulatory Commission, the costs of electricity have been calculated to be at a level of above 7,000 Rs. per year. This would exceed those for each of the other input factors of production. Furthermore, dry-land and groundwater-dependent agriculture has to compete on a common commodities market with farming systems based on canal irrigation which pay between 100 and 200 Rs. per acre and season for irrigation (AP Water Tax Act 1988).

The absence of marginal costs has led to highly energy-inefficient groundwater irrigation. Fortunately, incentives in agriculture for higher electricity quality are given, which can be combined with energy efficiency measures. The costs for repair and maintenance are mainly induced through low infrastructure quality. Effective measures are most feasible at the level of the electricity sub-station, isolating an agricultural electricity feeder and the connected distribution transformers.

Based on the Background studies and the Stakeholder analyses of WP 3.2 (Deb, Garg and Rommel 2009, Janetschek, Kimmich and Rommel 2009, Janetschek, Rommel and Kimmich 2009, Kimmich, Janetschek and Rommel 2009), this report has laid the foundations for understanding the economic incentives on the farm level. This serves as a prerequisite for the design of pilot projects and capacity development measures. The next step is to evaluate economic and institutional requirements of a set of alternative options of development measures, which will most likely enable a path of energy efficiency and mitigation of climate change. These options will then be tested for transferability and the actual and potential impediments and drivers of scaling up the approaches.

References

APERC. "Wheeling Tariffs Fy2009-10 to Fy2013-14 and Retail Supply Tariffs FY2009-10."

APTRANSCO. 2008. "Administration Report 2007-2008. Transmission Corporation of Andhra Pradesh Limited and Ap Distribution Companies." In *Tenth Administration Report*. Hyderabad.

Bhattacharyya, Subhes C. 2005. "The Electricity Act 2003: Will It Transform the Indian Power Sector?" *Utilities Policy* 13(3): 260–272.

Bhattacharyya, Subhes C., and Leena Srivastava. 2009. "Emerging Regulatory Challenges Facing the Indian Rural Electrification Programme." *Energy Policy* 37(1): 68–79.

Birner, Regina, Surupa Gupta, Neeru Sharma, and Nethra Palaniswamy. 2007. "The Political Economy of Agricultural Policy Reform in India. The Case of Fertilizer Supply and Electricity Supply for Groundwater Irrigation." 207. New Delhi and Washington: IFPRI.

Census of India. 2001. *Census of India, 2001. Series 1, India. Paper*. New Delhi: Office of Registrar General & Census Commissioner.

Chhibber, Pradeep K., and Ken Kollman. 2004. *The Formation of National Party Systems : Federalism and Party Competition in Canada, Great Britain, India, and the United States*. Princeton, N.J.: Princeton University Press.

CMIE. 2008. "Economic Intelligence Service - Energy, November 2008." edited by Centre for Monitoring Indian Economy. Mumbai.

Commons, John R. 1931. "Institutional Economics." *The American Economic Review* 21(4): 648–657.

Commons, John R. 1936. "Institutional Economics." *The American Economic Review* 26(1): 237–249.

Crew, Michael A., and Paul R. Kleindorfer. 2002. "Regulatory Economics: Twenty Years of Progress?" *Journal of Regulatory Economics* 21(1): 5–22.

Das, Keshab. 2007. "Electricity and Rural Development Linkage." In *Governance of Rural Electricity Systems in India*, edited by Haribandhu Panda and Institute of Rural Management (*Anand India), 53–66. New Delhi: Academic Foundation.

Deb, Kaushik, Anjali Garg, and Kai Rommel. 2009. "Background Study - Energy Management for the Emerging Megacity Hyderabad: Studying Demand, Supply and Gaps and Exploring Technical, Social and Institutional Factors." In *Sustainable Hyderabad Project Deliverable*. Berlin.

Dubash, Navroz K., and Sudhir Chella Rajan. 2000. "Power Politics: Process of Power Sector Reform in India." *Economic & Political Weekly* 36(35): 3367–3390.

Dubash, Navroz K., and D. Narasimha Rao. 2008. "Regulatory Practice and Politics: Lessons from Independent Regulation in Indian Electricity." *Utilities Policy* 16(4): 321–331.

Fan, Shenggen;, Ashok; Gulati, and Sukhadeo; Thorat. 2007. "Investment, Subsidies, and Pro-Poor Growth in Rural India." In *IFPRI Discussion Papers,* edited by IFPRI. Washington. New Delhi.

Ghoshal, Sumantra, and Peter Moran. 1996. "Bad for Practice: A Critique of the Transaction Cost Theory." *The Academy of Management Review* 21(1): 13–47.

Hagedorn, Konrad. 2008. "Particular Requirements for Institutional Analysis in Nature-Related Sectors." *Eur Rev Agric Econ* 35(3): 357–384.

Janetschek, Hannah, Christian Kimmich, and Kai Rommel. 2009. "Stakeholder Analysis for the Food-Water-Energy-Environment Nexus for Andhra Pradesh and Hyderabad." In *Sustainable Hyderabad Project Deliverable.* Berlin.

Janetschek, Hannah, Kai Rommel, and Christian Kimmich. 2009. "Background Study on the Food-Water-Energy-Environment Nexus in Urban and Peri-Urban Hyderabad." In *Sustainable Hyderabad Project Deliverable.* Berlin.

Kale, Sunila S. 2004. "Current Reforms: The Politics of Policy Change in India's Electricity Sector." *Pacific Affairs* 77(3): 467–491.

Kalra, Prem K., Rajiv Shekhar, and Vinod K. Shrivastava. 2007. "Electrification and Bio-Energy Options in Rural India." In *India Infrastructure Report, 2007 : Rural Infrastructure,* edited by 3iNetwork (India) and Infrastructure Development Finance Company (India), xxiii, 317 p. New Delhi ; New York: Oxford University Press.

Kimmich, Christian, Hannah Janetschek, and Kai Rommel. 2009. "The Energy Sector in Andhra Pradesh and Hyderabad: A Stakeholder Analysis: Unpublished." In *Sustainable Hyderabad Project Deliverable.* Berlin.

Modi, Vijay. 2005. "Improving Electricity Services in Rural India." In *Working Paper Series,* edited by The Earth Institute at Columbia University. Columbia: Center on Globalization and Sustainable Development.

Mohan, Rama, and N Sreekumar. 2009. "Evolving an Intregrated Approach for Improving Energy Efficiency of Ground Water Pumping for Agriculture Using Electricity: A Few Pointers from the Field." In *Discussion Paper.* Pune, Hyderabad: Prayas Energy Group, Centre for World Solidarity.

Newbery, David M. G. 1999. *Privatization, Restructuring, and Regulation of Network Utilities, Walras-Pareto Lectures.* Cambridge, Mass.: MIT Press.

Ostrom, Elinor. 2005. *Understanding Institutional Diversity.* Princeton, Oxford: Princeton University Press.

Powell, Walter W. 1991. "Neither Market nor Hierarchy: Network Forms of Organization." In *Markets, Hierarchies and Networks. The Coordination of Social Live*, edited by Grahame Thompson, Jennifer Frances, Rosalind Levacic and Jeremy Mitchell. London: SAGE.

Rao, S L. 2004. *Governing Power: A New Institution of Governance: The Experience with Independent Regulation of Electricity.* New Delhi: TERI.

Rothermund, Dietmar. 1993. *An Economic History of India : From Pre-Colonial Times to 1991.* 2nd ed. London ; New York: Routledge.

Sabatier, Paul A. 2007. *Theories of the Policy Process.* 2nd. ed. Boulder, Colo.: Westview Press.

Scharpf, Fritz Wilhelm. 1997. *Games Real Actors Play : Actor-Centered Institutionalism in Policy Research, Theoretical Lenses on Public Policy.* Boulder, Colo.: Westview Press.

Scott, C., and T. Shah. 2004. "Groundwater Overdraft Reduction through Agricultural Energy Policy: Insights from India and Mexico." *International Journal of Water Resources Development* 20: 149–164.

Shelanski, Howard A., and Peter G. Klein. 1995. "Empirical Research in Transaction Cost Economics: A Review and Assessment." *Journal of Law, Economics, & Organization* 11(2): 335–361.

Sinha, Aseema. 2004. "The Changing Political Economy of Federalism in India: A Historical Institutionalist Approach." *India Review* 3(1): 25–63.

Suri, K.C. 2002. *Democratic Process and Electoral Politics in Andhra Pradesh, India.* Vol. 180, *Working Paper.* London: Overseas Development Institute.

Thatcher, Mark. 2002. "Delegation to Independent Regulatory Agencies: Pressures, Functions and Contextual Mediation." *West European Politics* 25(1): 125–147.

Tongia, Rahul. 2007. "The Political Economy of Indian Power Sector Reforms." In *The Political Economy of Power Sector Reform: The Experiences of Five Major Developing Countries*, edited by David G. Victor and Thomas C. Heller, xviii, 330 p. Cambridge ; New York: Cambridge University Press.

Wilson, Robert. 2002. "Architecture of Power Markets." *Econometrica* 70(4): 1299–1340.

World Bank. 2001. "India: Power Supply to Agriculture. Volume 1: Summary Report." World Bank.